KEEP CALM AND COLOR ON

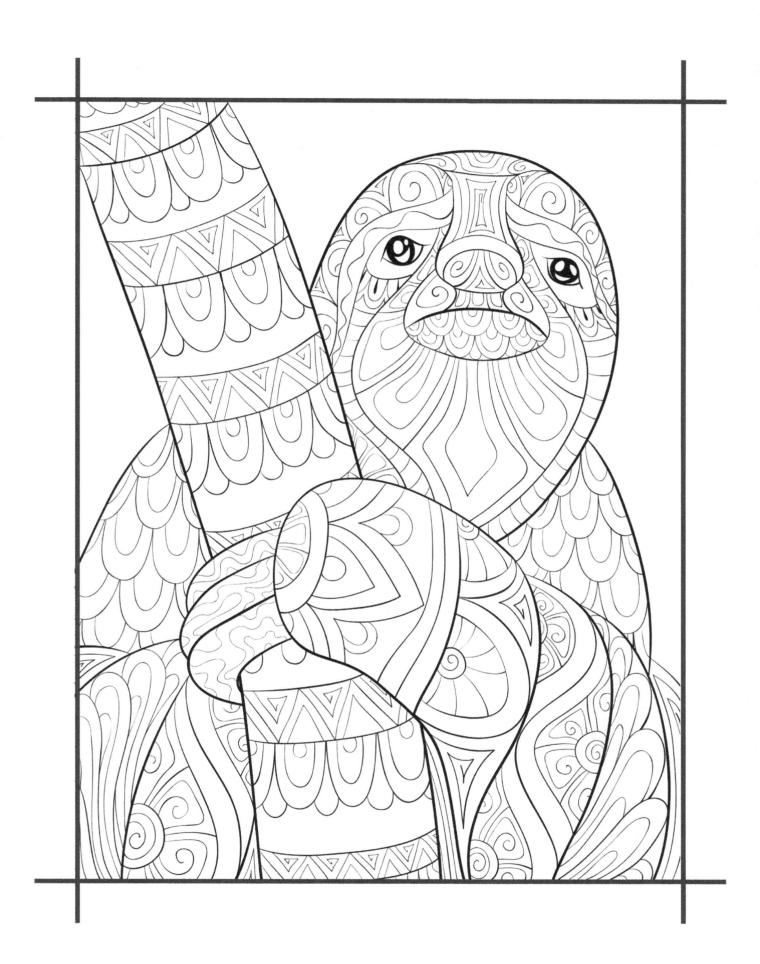

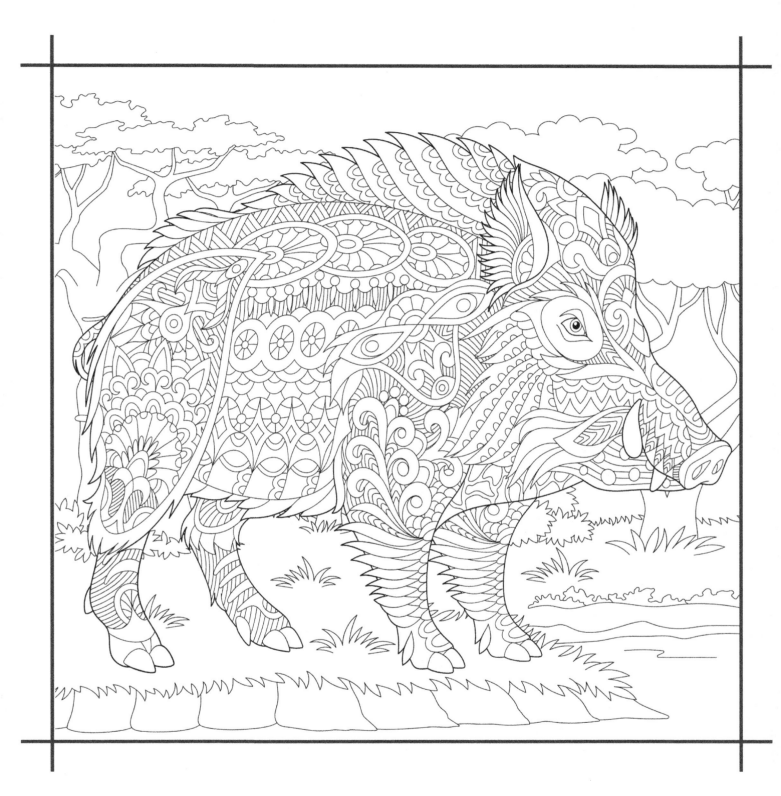

A Note from the Publisher

THANK YOU FOR BUYING THIS COLORING BOOK AND FOR SUPPORTING OUR SMALL BUSINESS. YOU ARE AMAZING!

I HOPE YOU ENJOY THIS BOOK AS MUCH I ENJOYED CREATING IT!

My name is Olympia, wife, and mother of 2 beautiful girls (my inspiration).

As a small family business, we are very dependent on reviews. Please consider leaving a review on Amazon and it would be greatly appreciated!
If you are not happy with this book, please write us an e-mail at customercare@jojo-kids.com

Check my Amazon Store for more unique products :

www.amazon.com/jojookids

Follow me on Instagram
@olympia.soares

Made in the USA
Monee, IL
21 June 2021